DIVINE PROTECTION & IMMUNITY WHILE SLEEPING

"...While Men Slept His Enemy came and Sowed Tares among the Wheat and Went his Way..."

PRAYER M. MADUEKE

PRAYER PUBLICATIONS
UNITED STATES

Copyright © 2021 Prayer M. Madueke

All rights reserved. No part of this work may be reproduced or transmitted in any form or by any means without written permission from the publisher unless otherwise indicated, all Scripture quotations are taken from the King James Version of the Bible, and used by permission. All emphasis within quotations is the author's additions.

ISBN: 979-8593671363

Published by **Prayer Publications**

259 Wainwright Street, Newark,

New Jersey 07112 United States.

From the Author

Prayer M. Madueke
CHRISTIAN AUTHOR

My name is Prayer Madueke. I'm a spiritual warrior in the Lord's vineyard. An accomplished author, speaker and expert on spiritual warfare and deliverance. I have published well over 100 books on every area of successful Christian living. I'm an acclaimed family and relationship counselor with several of titles dealing with those critical areas in the lives of the children of God. I travel to several countries each year speaking and conducting deliverance, breaking the yokes of demonic oppression and setting captives free.

I will be delighted to partner with you also in organized crusades, ceremonies, marriages and marriage seminars, special events, church ministration and fellowship for the advancement of God's kingdom here on earth.

All my books can be found <u>Amazon.com</u>. Visit my website <u>www.madueke.com</u> for powerful devotionals and materials.

Free Book Gift

Just to say Thank You for getting my book: Divine Protection and Immunity while Sleeping, I'll like to give you these books for free:

The link to download them are at the end of this book.

Your testimonies will abound. Click here to see my other books. They have produced many testimonies and I want your testimony to be one too.

Prayer Requests or Counselling

Send me an email on prayermadu@yahoo.com if you need prayers or counsel or you have questions. Better still if you want to be friends with me.

Table of Contents

1. Introduction 1
2. **Different Types Of Dream** 3
   Dreams From God 3
   Dreams from the Devil 8
   Witchcraft Dreams 10
   Consequences of Unreversed Witchcraft Dreams 14
   Some Dreams to Take Note Off 19

3. **Attacks from Determined Enemy** 28

DECREE SECTION

1. Decrees for Entrance to Divine Immunity 41
2. Decrees for Deliverance from Dream Harasments 43
3. Decrees for Deliverance from Dream Perversions 47

Introduction

No matter the battles, the spirit of darkness cannot defeat a Christian that bombards his destiny with the word of God. This is particularly true especially when you obtain total victory in your dreams. However, it is true that many things happen during our sleep, most of them are being played in our dreams oftentimes to make us aware of the danger ahead of us. Persistent evil attacks come from night hours during our sleep especially from 12am downward. If you want to have a sound sleep and also a good dream, a sleep without any horrible feelings, then reading your Bible and being prayerful can do a whole lot of good.

All other scriptures are very powerful, but reading the book of Psalms will also help you a lot in your warfare battles with your enemies. The examples of many that died in their sleep are too shocking to hear these days. There are many cases of people that sleep and die. Lots of people have received mysterious attacks during the night hours while others wake up to mild sickness, disappointments, unstable spirit, terrified, troubles, and to devastating attacks. This is not a great sign for any child of God. No wonder the Bible says, in Psalms 4:8: "I will both lay me down in peace, and sleep: for thou, LORD, only makest me dwell in safety." In this chapter we will taka closer look at what happens during sleep. There are different types of dreams.

CHAPTER ONE
Different Types Of Dream

Dreams From God

A lot of activities both good and bad go on while people sleep without their knowledge and their permission. Most times, these things happen while we sleep through dreams as a result of series of thoughts, images or emotions that occur while we sleep. Dream is an activity observed or enacted in one's sleep and impressed in one's memory so that when one wakes up at times can be remembered vividly and can be relayed. Dreams that come from God is to warn his children of an impending danger, to inform his children on what to do, secrets of success. Dreams that come from God points to the victim of God's future plans, what to do, to warn him of the dangers ahead, what to do to prevent the evil plans of the devil and his agents.

The dream that God showed to Joseph (Genesis 37:1-10) was about what will happen to him in the future, how great he was going to be, God's plan. God warned the three wise men in the dream not to return to Herod. In the dream also, God appeared to Joseph, the husband of Mary, the mother of Jesus to flee into Egypt and stay there until the next information comes. The reason was that Herod was planning to kill Jesus at that time, so without wasting any time, Joseph left that very night to Egypt. Joseph was spiritual enough to hear God's voice but other parents who were spiritual deaf lost their children. All the spiritual deaf parents in the coast of Bethlehem lost their children from the age of two to a day old (Matthew 2:12-16). A dream is a spiritual monitor in the spirit world. It is a supernatural way through which God speaks to His people. God must have spoken to other parents but either they were deaf spiritually or that their memory to remember dreams was weak, under satanic attack.

Dreams can come as an activity that you are involved in. It can also come as an event. Dreams also can come in form of a message to some people. It can also come as an attack on the dreamer. If dreams are not remembered it could bring disaster. It is a common experience for most people that their dreams are often forgotten and difficult to recall. Believers should take dreams seriously, but on the other hand, we are not to put our confidence in dreams. Our confidence should be in the word of God.

God spoke to people (believers and unbelievers) through dreams in the past and still does so today. However, we must check every idea, thought, or dream with the word of God. Secondly, we must pray seriously after dreams and commit all things to God.

God-given dreams can encourage believers in a particular situation, to warn you, enter into covenant with you, to correct you, direct you or to extend his blessing to you. It is not all the activity in the dream that comes from the devil, even some eating or drinking.

> *And as he lay and slept under a juniper tree, behold, then an angel touched him, and said unto him, Arise and eat. And he looked, and, behold, there was a cake baken on the coals, and a cruse of water at his head. And he did eat and drink, and laid him down again. And the angel of the LORD came again the second time, and touched him, and said, Arise and eat; because the journey is too great for thee. And he arose, and did eat and drink, and went in the strength of that meat forty days and forty nights unto Horeb the mount of God. - **1 Kings 19:5-8***

Believers must have a good relationship with God to attract good dreams from God. In times of battle, spiritual conflict against a physical stronger enemy, an organized witch or wizard, determined enemy, you must be spiritual alive to hear from God. The sacrifices of four hundred and fifty prophets of Baal did not bring down fire to consume their sacrifices from morning till noon. There was no voice or any that answered, even when they cried aloud, cut themselves with knives and lancets till blood gushed out (1 Kings 18:25-29).

Though their sacrifices couldn't bring down fire to consume the burn the wood, the stones and the dust but it did something later against the man of God, Elijah.

> *And he came thither unto a cave, and lodged there; and, behold, the word of the LORD came to him, and he said unto him, What doest thou here, Elijah? And he said, I have been very jealous for the LORD God of hosts: for the children of Israel have forsaken thy covenant, thrown down thine altars, and slain thy prophets with the sword; and I, even I only, am left; and they seek my life, to take it away… And he said, I have been very jealous for the LORD God of hosts: because the children of Israel have forsaken thy covenant, thrown down thine altars, and slain thy prophets with the sword; and I, even I only, am left; and they seek my life, to take it away.* **– 1 Kings 19: 9-10, 14**

Elijah was a great prophet; called, anointed and empowered by God. But the sacrifices of the four hundred and fifty prophets of Baal plus the threats for the mother of witchcraft Jezebel put him to fear. The demons invoked during the evil sacrifices entered into Jezebel to threaten him, and he left his servant to run for his life. After a whole day's journey into the wilderness he requested to die and asked God to take away his life. At that point, what he needed was spiritual food, the food of the champions that only God can provide and that was what he got that night (1 Kings 19:1-8). At his weak time, if he was not a believer, under divine mercy, the witches would have fed him that night instead of God. Before that night, before he went to sleep, his immunity both spiritual and physical was down, very low and if the witchcraft demons invoked by the four hundred and fifty had fed him, he would have died before morning. But God out of his sheer mercy, fed him with spiritual food, the food of the champions and he went in the strength of that food for forty days and forty nights.

Dreams from the Devil

Dreams from the devil afflicts with sickness, deceives and confuses, kill, steal or destroy. It is more dangerous when you do not dream at all. It means that you are ignorant of both God's plan and the devils. If you know the will of God and also learn the acts of prayer after dreams, the deceiver of this age will not deceive you. The deceivers in Babylon took advantage of the superstitions in their days to make much money through false interpretation of dreams. We should be cautious about deceivers around us today (Daniel 2:4-11).

When Nebuchadnezzar turned to the occult in his apprehension of future calamities, he was greatly disappointed. In our dreams, whether they are positive or negative, we should turn to God in prayer. Some people are careless over their dreams while some are in fear, panic, worry and in anxiety. But true believers should confront every dream with the word of God and prayers.

We should confidently face the enemy by wisely opposing him with the true word of God and fervent prayers. In times of any opposing dream, troubles and trying circumstances, we must be composed and calm, using the weapons of prayer instead of fear. When Daniel was confronted by the dreams of the king, he communed with the King of Kings. His reaction during such crises was courage, consciousness of God's presence, and prayer (Daniel 2:17-19).

The purpose of this book is to enable you know the right prayers to pray in every situation. It will help to speed up the good things in your dreams into manifestations. It will also aid you to convert bad dreams into good ones and make you a winner in your dreams and not a looser.

Witchcraft Dreams

Witchcraft dreams are the dreams that come from the devil, or the kingdom of darkness to bewitch an individual. It is a dream designed to pull someone away from God; His plans and promises. It is a dream meant to initiate one unconsciously into an evil group in order to afflict such a person, even unto death.

Dream covenants have been used by the devil and his agents to oppress both Christians and non-Christians in all the nations of the world. It can also be used to bring two contradicting or opposing persons together in common agreement to fulfil certain obligations. It is designed to bring people together to fight common battles in the spirit unconsciously.

Once the devil or his agents involve you in a particular thing in your dreams consciously or unconsciously you become a victim, subject to some unknown powers. The agents of dream covenant make their victims to abide by what they agreed in their dreams even to some physical agents. A friendship established in the spirit during dreams is binding in the physical also.

An agreement in the spirit during dream is meant to control the physical agreement unless you understand how to deal with evil dream covenants. Witches and wizards can also use dreams to misplace people's destinies. They use magical and mysterious powers in the spirit to cause wickedness to people in the dreams. They can skilfully manipulate people in the dream to do evil things. Witches and wizards feed people in the dreams with all manner of evil food. When people are manipulated to eat demonic food in the dream their lives are corrupted, defiled and polluted; thereby unable to please God physically.

Evil experiences in the dream cause people to live a contradictory life to God and his Word. People who are bewitched in the dream to any action are deceived to misbehave physically. They are evils determined to lead them against God. That is why believers should take immediate action against any evil that took place against them in the dream.

The devil uses his agents to plant evil into people lives in the dreams. If those evil plantations are not dealt with in prayers, they can be disastrous. Witches and wizards plant the spirit of seduction in people's lives in the dreams. Evil plantations in the dreams can cause people to conspire, gossip, and fight against God's constituted authorities. Witches and wizards plant the spirits of adultery, fornication, unfaithfulness to God, pretence, unforgiving spirits, murder, etc., through the dream into people's lives.

When an intelligent person suddenly begins to fail exams, an evil seed has been planted into his life in the dream. When a person's progress is blocked by some powers, an evil seed has been planted in the dream against him. When a peaceful marriage or home begins to have crisis; an evil has been planted. When your concentration is under distractions, an evil visitor had visited your dreams. If you don't deal with witchcraft dreams, your physical and spiritual immunity will be reduced. At that point, you will not have even the physical strength to resist ordinary sickness, temptations and daily trials. When the agent of the devil attacks you with food in the dream and you forget the dream or may not even know that anything took place, you are in trouble. Through constant eating from satanic source without you knowing, you will be reduced to certain lusts, evil desires or a real act of sin.

Some victims will experience sudden spiritual backwardness, backsliding, constant failures, financial problems, bad health, prayerlessness, depression, mysterious situations, strange sickness, and frustration. Others will be attacked with confusion, deprivation of right, sudden disaster, great loss, sudden death of good things and loss of great opportunities. If they still fail to do something, pray the right prayers, they may enter into another stage called, inexplicable poverty, mysterious accidents, hatred and rejections without reason.

Some may be attacked with late marriage, oppressions, occultism, initiations, witchcraft, evil sacrifices to escape their shame and reproaches. In their frustrations, they will be engaged with unreasonable quarrelling, fear, bitterness, anger, jealousy, worry and anxiety. If they still remain in their ignorance, fighting wrongly, selfishness, rebellion, unclean sexual thoughts, drunkenness and addictions to many unholy things will set in. Witchcraft dreams can bring barrenness, mysterious abortions, mis-marriage, failure to menstruate, irregular Menstruation and can lead to multiple problems.

It can lead to fibroid, cancer, tumour, loss of good job, loss of life and eternal life in hell fire with the devil. For some Christians who doesn't believe in dreams or under the manipulation of satanic dreams a witch or just an envious agent of the devil can be feeding them gradually.

When a witch or wizard wants to terminate your health, he can just feed you in the dream. With a simple spoon of food in the dream, your life may be corrupted. A corrupted life in the dream can stop you from enjoying your Christian life, prevent you from pursuing a good venture to a successful end; causing you to meet setbacks in many areas of your life. It can also bring irritation and vagabond spirit into your life, cause you to dream of water, and make easy things difficult for your life. A single sex in your dream or any evil action can cause you non-achievement, termination of prosperous business, painful menstruation, untimely death, blockage of menstruation, prolonged pregnancy, prolong labour and delivery through caesareans.

Many undiagnosed and incurable diseases came into people lives as a result of witchcraft dreams.

Consequences of Unreversed Witchcraft Dreams

- Un-reversed evil dream can discover destinies and waste them.

- They can bring problems into marriages and cause divorce.

- It can afflict people from birth to the grave.

- It can lead people into terrible wrong decisions.

- It can put people's progress to a standstill and bring their goals in life to a waste.

- It can lead people to seek for help in a wrong place.

- It can close down good doors and waste great opportunities and greatness.

- It can weaken people and cause them to be tired of life.

- It can cause people to engage in a useless project.

- It can promote poverty and lack; keeping victims in debts unto death.

- It can make people's lives worthless; cause war and famine.

- It can plant evil into people's lives and cause them to suffer.

- It can take people out of God's plan and promises.

- It can limit people; causing them to suffer and struggle in vain in life.

- It can lead people to take wrong decisions in marriage, and make them to marry their enemies.

- An unchallenged evil/witchcraft dream can remove people's hope and cause them to accept defeats.

- It can place people under a curse and keep them in problems for life.

- An unchallenged witchcraft dream can kill, bury its victim, and send him to hell eternally.

- You can be marked for evil through witchcraft dreams.

- Your destiny can be harvested by your enemy through evil dreams.

- Your business, marriage, etc., can be caged through evil dreams.

- Your brain can be damaged through evil dream.

- Your womb can be locked-up through witchcraft dreams attacks.

- Your organs can be paralysed through evil dreams.

- A person can be demoted through evil dreams.

- Your life, progress, marriage can expire through evil dreams.

- The water spirit can suck your destiny when you fail to challenge their witchcraft dream.

- An embargo can be placed against your destiny through dreams.

- Through witchcraft dreams destinies can be arrested.

- Blessing can be diverted through witchcraft dreams.
- Lives can be weakened and detained spiritually through witchcraft dreams.
- Investments can be wasted, scattered and ceased through witchcraft dreams.
- Lives and greatness can be spiritually imprisoned through witchcraft dream.
- A young person can be made old, confused and mad through witchcraft dream.
- People who are born to be great can be cursed through witchcraft dreams.
- Anything bad can take place when witchcraft dreams are left unchallenged.
- Witchcraft dream can put a cigarette in your left hand and a bottle of bear in your right hand.
- You can be forced to reject your blessing through witchcraft dream.
- Witches and wizards can give you evil loads through witchcraft dream.
- A single sex in the dream, or feeding can programme into your life the spirit of compulsory stealing, smoking, fornication or a particular bad habit.

- An unchallenged witchcraft dream can give you an evil partner in your family.
- Impossibility can come into people's life through evil dream.

Finally, witchcraft dreams can be converted to blessing through prayers. You can look at the prayer list and pray against the evil dreams that usually affect your life. You can as well pray them after having the dream. Undoubtedly, the prayers in this book will convert your bad dreams to good dreams. Your vision and dream will change for the better. In your dreams, you will no longer see evil nor your enemies and if you must see them, they will bow in defeat to you. You will be victorious in your dream from today. From today, when you dream, you will remember them. If God allows you to see defeat in your dreams, the purpose is for you to know what the enemy has planned to do in your life.

If God allows you to see the evil dream at all, the purpose is for you to pray against it and convert them to good dreams. From today, the Lord will draw the curtain aside for you to have a glimpse of heaven, the eternal city. When you begin to see this eternal city in your dreams, your conviction will change because heaven cannot be stained with sin. It is a transparent city, clear as crystal. I decree that from this moment our dreams and visions shall change for good towards heaven. For those who want a change and desire victory over witchcraft dreams, Jesus must be honoured in their lives. They must be born again and remain faithful to the end.

> *"And the Spirit and the bride say, Come. And let him that heareth say, Come. And let him that is athirst come. And whosoever will, let him take the water of life freely"* (**Revelation 22:17**).

If you fail to claim the good things you receive in your dreams, they may elude you physically. Likewise, if you fail to cancel the bad thing in your dreams, they may manifest physically.

Some Dreams to Take Note Off

To see animals in your dream generally gives you a clue to the spiritual challenges coming against you. It depends on the type of animal you see in your dream, but the type of animal you see will give you an idea, the kind of battle going on in your life and help you to pray the right prayers. When you see a dog fighting you, biting you or barking at you in the dream, immediately you wake up, you need to pray against lusts, sexual sin, unclean and immoral thoughts, and sexual perversions like fornication or adultery.

Serpents in the dreams will likely bring satanic poisons that lead to violence, wickedness, destructions or death. An agent of the devil, occult enemy can meet a witchdoctor to perform a sacrifice to invoke a familiar spirit from your place of birth.

> *And he brought him into the field of Zophim, to the top of Pisgah, and built seven altars, and offered a bullock and a ram on every altar… He hath not beheld iniquity in Jacob, neither hath he seen perverseness in Israel: the LORD his God is with him, and the shout of a king is among them. God brought them out of Egypt; he hath as it were the strength of an unicorn. Surely there is no enchantment against Jacob, neither is there any divination against Israel: according to this time it shall be said of Jacob and*

of Israel, What hath God wrought! – **Numbers 23:14, 21-23**

An intelligent witchdoctor will not just agree to perform a sacrifice against anyone without checking the person's relationship with God. If you convince him to do so, it will not work and may likely backfire. So, what they will first do is to separate you from God before they go into the sacrifice, and if they succeed, they can attack you by feeding you in the dream or even physically. When Balak invited Balaam and bribed him to offer a sacrifice against the children of Israel, the sacrifices failed because the children of Israel were committed to God (Numbers 23:6, 17, 21).

In the day of the sacrifices in twenty-one altars, all the princes of Moab were committed to see the children of Israel destroyed. When the sacrifices failed over and over, while all the princes were standing, their King Balak asked what hath the LORD spoken, meaning, "Why can't we succeed?" Balaam answered, "Because the demons invoked in the twenty-one altars did not behold iniquity in Jacob, neither hath he seen perversion in Israel."

So, if you want to have divine protection and immunity, avoid iniquity, sin and perversion while sleeping or awake. There is a man called great Leonard and his half-brother, very occultic, wicked and destructive called Sandey Egbuaba, a police officer retired. After killing others around him through occult means tried in vain to eliminate the great Leonard, he looked at him and said, "I know what to do". Great Leo asked him, what are you going to do? He said, I will deliver you into a woman to separate you from God, then I will strike and you will go the way of others. Leo told me and I advised him to be born again and to be very careful with women and sin, especially sexual sin. The first thing that happened was that the wife of Great Leo just got tired of their marriage, dropped her two young small children and went to Northern state for prostitution.

At that point, great Leo entered into trouble, his finances were attacked and everywhere he went to, beautiful women beg him for sex. Some midnights, Leo will call me to pray for him because all his body will be ripe to commit immorality and the girls are readily waiting for his consent. It was a very long battle, but because of the advance knowledge, Leo was a bit carful, especially knowing whom his half-brother Sandey, Egbuaba is. The battle is still on but we believe God that the enemy will fail and bow.

After twenty-one evil sacrifices in different evil altar, Balaam gave Balak a counsel on how to destroy Israel to stop their journey of life.

> *And Balaam said unto Balak, build me here seven altars, and prepare me here seven oxen and seven rams. And Balak did as Balaam had spoken; and Balak and Balaam*

offered on every altar a bullock and a ram... And Balak said unto him, Come, I pray thee, with me unto another place, from whence thou mayest see them: thou shalt see but the utmost part of them, and shalt not see them all: and curse me them from thence. And he brought him into the field of Zophim, to the top of Pisgah, and built seven altars, and offered a bullock and a ram on every altar. –
Numbers 23:1-2, 13-14

In the first seven altars which represent perfection and no escape, Balaam, Balak, the princes and every occult people in Moab failed to destroy the children of Israel in their evil altars. They went to another dangerous place; a place of higher multiple altars where the whole Israel can be gathered in an evil altar and be cursed. If an occult person, a wicked person fails to kill you, he will try to curse you, your children, marriage, business or anything in your life. So, they went to the field of Zophim; a place with multiple altars where a lot of people go to get a charm to curse people's greatness. In that field, many people are scattered with their evil priests, consulting demons in charge of curses but there is an exalted top in the center of the field.

There, occult grandmasters like Sandey were the only occult people and witchdoctors qualified to climb to offer sacrifices. It is an upstairs; a top called the top of Pisgah where no matter where an enemy is can be traced for a curse, an attack and destruction. When they got there, they built another seven altars, making it fourteen altars, and they started sacrificing, invoking, enchanting and divining but they failed again.

> *And Balak said unto Balaam, Come, I pray thee, I will bring thee unto another place; peradventure it will please God that thou mayest curse me them from thence. And Balak brought Balaam unto the top of Peor, that looketh toward Jeshimon. And Balaam said unto Balak, build me here seven altars, and prepare me here seven bullocks and seven rams. And Balak did as Balaam had said, and offered a bullock and a ram on every altar.* – **Numbers 23:27-30**

If you have a single determined enemy in your family; an unbeliever who consults a witchdoctor, a colleague in an office or any agent of Satan who hates you, you must be very prayerful. So, after they failed at Zophim, the top of Pisgah in the seven altars, making it fourteen, they proceeded to the most dangerous altar at that time. This time around they went to Peor; a place that looked toward an evil bush inhabiting dangerous demons called Jeshimon, and climbed the top of it. How powerful they are, they built another seven altars, making it twenty-one altars and sacrifices were again given to evil spirits to waste a whole innocent nation.

Unfortunately for them, the children of Israel were still innocent, no iniquity and perversion in their relationship with God, so God was among them, protecting them. In their sleeps, there was no iniquity before they went to bed. Whether they were sleeping or awake, there was no iniquity, no perversion, the LORD their God was with them. They had divine protection, divine immunity and powerful divine presence, so enemies' divinations, evil summons, divinations and multiple enchantments against them failed. After failure in the twenty-one altars in the land of Moab, in the field of Zophim, at the top of Pisgah, at Peor's top opposite an evil bush, towards Jeshimon, Balaam gave Balak an evil counsel.

> *But I have a few things against thee, because thou hast there them that hold the doctrine of Balaam, who taught Balac to cast a stumbling block before the children of Israel, to eat things sacrificed unto idols, and to commit fornication. –* **Revelation 2:14**

> *And Israel abode in Shittim, and the people began to commit whoredom with the daughters of Moab. And they called the people unto the sacrifices of their gods: and the people did eat, and bowed down to their gods. And Israel*

joined himself unto Baalpeor: and the anger of the LORD was kindled against Israel. –Numbers 25:1-3

Balaam counseled Balak to give contracts to all the best reigning worldly fashion designers in Moab to sow worldly dress for the most beautiful daughter of Moab. The clothes must be slack, shirt like, topless, backless, mini, perforated, very transparent and body exposing. After that, the selected marine possessed ladies, very beautiful and charming went to Shittim, where the children of Israel camped and seduced them. They fed them with the foods and meat used to offer sacrifices to the twenty-one altars and joined them spiritually and physically in an evil relationship. Unknown to many people some evil altars, even the ones consulted many years ago by our ancestors can retain words spoken to them for many years. At your weak moment monitoring demons from those altars can report you for an attack unless you are prayerful and learn how to withdraw things from evil altars.

When the children of Israel committed whoredom and immorality with the daughters of Moab, God withdrew from their midst. Their lives were exposed for demonic attacks. Their security was broken, they lost divine protection, and divine immunity, and demons from twenty-one altars attacked them. Under such situation, they despised the preachings of Moses and the elders to mix up with modern styles of Moab. Every good thing in them – business, true worships, respect to elders, etc. started dying, including human beings. All the youth lost good relationship with God, except one young youth called Phinehas.

> *And, behold, one of the children of Israel came and brought unto his brethren a Midianitish woman in the sight of Moses, and in the sight of all the congregation of the children of Israel, who were weeping before the door of the tabernacle of the congregation. And when Phinehas, the son of Eleazar, the son of Aaron the priest, saw it, he rose up from among the congregation, and took a javelin in his hand; And he went after the man of Israel into the tent, and thrust both of them through, the man of Israel, and the woman through her belly. So, the plague was stayed from the children of Israel. And those that died in the plague were twenty and four thousand.* **– Numbers 25:6-9**

But before Phinehas intervened, twenty-four thousand people have died. From the plague and what twenty-one altars failed to do, immorality did it. For those who are asking me, write a book that will give us protection and divine immunity, this is my reply: Stay away from sin and learn spiritual warfare by putting on the whole armor even after staying away from sin (Numbers 23:21-23; Ephesians 6:10-11, 13).

CHAPTER TWO

ATTACKS FROM DETERMINED ENEMY

I have been a missionary in the dark regions of West Africa, including many countries in Africa as a whole even to the western world. I have come under serious conflict, direct physical and spiritual confrontations with evil groups, satanic agents, determined and uncompromising enemies of the truth. Right from my family level, community set ups, cities and national evil group who profess solid faith in idolatry, witchcrafts and occultism, I was a target.

My survival, life today is by the grace of God. My assistant, Samuel Mensah was squeezed off life few minutes after I discussed with him by determined witchcraft group. Few minutes after our discussion on phone I received another call that he was gone, and like joke he was later committed to the mother death at Awudome cemetery. All the witches and wizards who vowed to destroy me were put to shame by the powers of the Almighty. These are determined enemies of the gospel in a community who will not take no for an answer until they achieve their aim.

> *And the same time there arose no small stir about that way. For a certain man named Demetrius, a silversmith, which made silver shrines for Diana, brought no small gain unto the craftsmen… Some therefore cried one thing, and some another: for the assembly was confused; and the more part knew not wherefore they were come together. –*
> **Acts 19:23-24, 32**

Agents of the devil, witches and wizards can organize witchcraft crusade, demonic revival and move people against you everywhere you go. They can mark their victim with the marks of hatred, fear, failures, defeats, accident, troubles and people will tell lies against you everywhere you go. Once the door of your life is opened through dreams attack, the creature will be raised against you everywhere you go and your life will be exposed to all manner of attack. A little feeding in the dream, drinks, sex or demonic involvement, immediately you wake up, your day, weeks, months or years of your life will be filled with crises, troubles and huge failures without reason. You will see people make themselves an enemy to you without knowing why and yourself will be surprised without getting an answer.

When Paul preached the true gospel and lived a pure life of holiness, the community witches raise people against him. At Ephesus, newly believer was empowered, multitudes repented, many miracles took place, many burnt their curious books but Demetrius was not happy. He was in charge of an occult group in the city and many of his cult members left their group for Christ. Because he bewitched the people in the city, locked them up spiritually in his altars and they were under his control. He went to the city altar and loosed people to rise against Paul and his evangelistic team. People were stirred up, were full of wrath, crying out saying, Great is Diana of the Ephesus and the whole city was filled with confusion. Many people left their offices, house, assignment and entered the street crying and shouting without knowing the reason why for the space of two hours. That is what we call in deliverance witchcraft crusade or revival.

Many people want to stop smoking, taking drugs, committing certain sin but they can't. They are bound in the community, city and personal altars of occult grand masters, making gain for them.

> *And it came to pass, as we went to prayer, a certain damsel possessed with a spirit of divination met us, which brought her masters much gain by soothsaying... And when her masters saw that the hope of their gains was gone, they caught Paul and Silas, and drew them into the marketplace unto the rulers –* **Acts 16:16, 19**

If your mouth is in the evil altar, you are bound to eat their food prepared spiritually in their altars. Any part of you that is in the evil altar is no longer under your control perfectly and that is why they can give you to a marriage spiritually without your permission. If you marry such a person physically even as a virgin, you will never enjoy such marriage because he or she was already married spiritually. That is the reason why many cannot get married at all, marry but separate, divorce or stay together physically as enemies. If such couple has children, they will never enjoy their children because spiritual spouse contributed in the formation of those babies from conception.

> *Thou shalt betroth a wife, and another man shall lie with her: thou shalt build an house, and thou shalt not dwell therein: thou shalt plant a vineyard, and shalt not gather the grapes thereof… Thou shalt beget sons and daughters, but thou shalt not enjoy them; for they shall go into captivity. – **Deuteronomy 28:30, 41***

That is why your cloth will be on you but they still enter your room without knocking and mess you up. If you wish to have divine protection and immunity while sleeping, even as a believer, minister of the gospel, you have to rise up and resist them.

> *Wherefore we would have come unto you, even I Paul, once and again; but Satan hindered us. – **1 Thessalonians 2:18***

> *Submit yourselves therefore to God. Resist the devil, and he will flee from you.* – **James 4:7**

It is true that once you get born again old things, things like what you are hearing now are meant to pass away. But such powers most of the time try to fight God's word. That is what Paul experienced and saw the same taking place in born again Christians and likened Christian life here on earth as warfare – fighting and wrestling. James' counsel to believers is to resist them and they will flee, and failure to do so brings defeat in a miserable way to true believers. That is why many beautiful, handsome believers are not married and the married are not enjoying their marriage. That was why Paul and his evangelistic team planned to enter the city of Thessalonians but were not able to enter. He planned to enter over and over, again and again but failed.

Even when he decided to go alone, Satan blocked his way and hindered him. We need to tell ourselves and the younger Christians the truth, there are satanic activities going on here on earth around us and we need to rise up to fight, wrestle and war against them.

> *But while men slept, his enemy came and sowed tares among the wheat, and went his way* - **Matthew 13:25**

What is the meaning of what Christ said in the above verse, while men slept, what kind of sleep is Christ talking about? You can sleep physically or spiritually and at that point, if you don't have divine immunity, a lot of evil investment, demonic plantation can take place.

A prayer-less believer, who lives in an evil invested area, may physically go to bed with weak immunity, and the enemy can invade his or her life. A backslidden believer can also sleep but his immunity cannot carry him or her all through the night or the time of sleeping. A living sinner, weak Christian, prayer-less believer may be awake but spiritually, he is sleeping and the enemy can as well plant evil even in the broad day light.

In times like this, deception, conspiracy, strife, betrayal, contention, multiplied opposition; oppressions, injustice, poverty, late marriage, trials and all manner of problem will show up and defeat such a person. But if you are a Christian, they may still come but they will not succeed.

> *But now thus saith the LORD that created thee, O Jacob, and he that formed thee, O Israel, Fear not: for I have redeemed thee, I have called thee by thy name; thou art mine. When thou passest through the waters, I will be with thee; and through the rivers, they shall not overflow thee:*

> *when thou walkest through the fire, thou shalt not be burned; neither shall the flame kindle upon thee.* – **Isaiah 43:1-2**

> *Many are the afflictions of the righteous: but the LORD delivereth him out of them all.* – **Psalms 34:19**

If you are loyal to God, faithful to Him, and know your right to his eternal, unchanging truth, his power will protect and preserve you. It may not be possible for some people to completely stop dream attack but God will not allow them to be destroyed. God did not promise us freedom from satanic attacks, but He promised to deliver us when the enemy attacks us. That is why He gave us the option to pray, seek Him, knock at his door and to resist the devil and he will flee. That is why He directed us to his only begotten son and Jesus said, come unto me to receive deliverance that gives rest.

Jesus is God's ark to every mankind, and only the people that obey His word and enter the ark will be saved. Christ as God's provided immunity says, I am the way, the truth and the life and without Him there is no life. If Noah had refused to enter the ark, he would have been destroyed just like others who ignored the call until the door of the ark was closed. If Lot had refused to join the angels of the LORD, and decide to remain in Sodom, he would have been burnt like others who ignored the call. If Joseph had refused to forgive his brethren, the chosen tribe would have died in hunger but he forgave them. Likewise, if you refuse to forgive your offenders, your immunity during sleep will not carry you through in times of attack.

If Phinehas has joined other youth of his time, the immunity of the nation would have been compromised, but he refused to join immoral friends to commit whoredom (Numbers 25:6-8). If you single yourself out from among sinners, your immunity can stay the plagues designed by the devil to wipe out your family, community or nation. When Esau despised his birth right, his immunity was reduced and instead of occupying the first position, he was pushed to second position.

> *Looking diligently lest any man fail of the grace of God; lest any root of bitterness springing up trouble you, and thereby many be defiled; Lest there be any fornicator, or profane person, as Esau, who for one morsel of meat sold his birthright. For ye know how that afterward, when he would have inherited the blessing, he was rejected: for he found no place of repentance, though he sought it carefully with tears. –**Hebrews 12:15-17***

Things that destroy immunity differs from person to person, family, community or environmental foundation. Some foundation promotes certain sin. So, everyone must check the sins and actions of his foundation or besetting sins that destroys spiritual and physical immunity. The sin or action that exposed Herod to worms was his murder of John the Baptist but that of Judas Iscariot was love of money. The thief in the left hand of Jesus insulted Christ and his spiritual immunity was exposed to death and destruction eternally in hell.

Everyone must check and do everything possible to avoid any evil character, weakness that can remove him or her from protection while sleeping. When the announcement of my transfer from a particular nation came up, the entire organized witchcraft network was very happy. The Lord used my ministry to disorganize them, and when I was about to leave, they cerebrated it. I was to hand over to the next minister in the morning after Sunday service, but the pastor missed his flight. Those witches didn't come to church in the morning to avoid hearing my sharp preaching, so they waited in the evening service to see the new pastor 's preaching. Unknown to them I was still around to minister in the evening also. That evening came and all the witches were very much around, rejoicing and waiting for the new pastor to mount the pulpit. While I was in the office, I was told what was going on outside. So, I prayed and God gave me a single Bible reference to preach with Ephesians 6:10.

Immediately I mounted the pulpit, it was like "Is this his ghost or the real Pastor Prayer Madueke?" I prayed and said, "The Lord said I should tell everyone here to be strong in the Lord, not in witchcraft." Everywhere was quiet and I continued and said, "Don't be strong in witchcraft because witchcraft is evil, enmity with God, abominable, hateful and unprofitable to God."

Some of them bent their head, sighed, stood up and walked out. So, as I said to them, I am saying the same thing to you: Don't be strong in doing anything that is sinful! Repent of all your sins and commit your life to doing right things. Avoid sin, iniquity and perversion and your life will not be exposed to satanic attacks and victory over dream attacks will be your portion. You can only be assured of divine protection and immunity while sleeping by living a righteous life. Make sure that before you start any day or retire to bed every night you are at peace with God and man.

> *Follow peace with all men, and holiness, without which no man shall see the Lord –* **Hebrews 12:14**
>
> *My little children, these things write I unto you, that ye sin not. And if any man sin, we have an advocate with the Father, Jesus Christ the righteous –* **1 John 2:1**

As you try your best to please God at all cost, do the right thing, forgive your offenders and live peaceful with all men with prayerfulness and humility, your immunity will be guaranteed. At that point, if you pray, God will answer and in times of attacks, oppressions, your prayer will help you to receive victory, no matter the size of your enemy. One of my friends and a relation, Sandey Egbuaba, half-brother of great Leo, very powerful wizard once promised to send fire to hurt me from what he called holy sanctuary. I truly understood him because I understand the terms occult people uses. That night he promised to attack me but I was equally ready by God's grace. Like a determined wizard he is, he started and I was bombarded with evil visitors from occult world with fearful steady demonic bullets from midnight till morning. At the end, the demons he invoked and sent to me, my family was rejected and they returned the arrows from his holy sanctuary beck. Like an experienced wizard, very tactful he dodged the arrows and the brain, mental storehouse of one of his most intelligent and beautiful daughters was affected (1 Samuel 19:4-5; 20:32).

The worse investment anyone can give his children is investment that will cause them to inherit enemy through wrong counsel, falsehood and getting them to take side with him, even when he is clearly wrong. All his family members were misled and they agree on whatever he tells them without enquiry, even the acclaimed learned ones among them. One of his sons once wrote to me, boasting of the people his father has killed, and promised to kill more. But I ignored him because he is under deceit heading to doom. However, the only way to overcome them is by having a good relationship with God, following peace with all men and being prayerful. So, if you are not born again, repented and forsaken all your known sins, do so now before we go into prayers.

DECREE SECTION

Decrees for Entrance to Divine Immunity

Every inherited iniquity in the root of my life, be destroyed, in the name of Jesus. You the sin nature reigning in my life, be destroyed forever by the blood of Jesus. I break and loose my life from every bondage of sin, in the name of Jesus. Blood of Jesus, flow into my foundation and destroy every root of sin. Everything standing between me and God, disappear forever, in the name of Jesus. I break and loose myself from every link connecting me to Satan and sin. Heavenly Father, empower me to hate sin with joy and happiness, in the name of Jesus. Any relationship between me and spirit being, break to pieces. Any spiritual armed robber organized to destroy my destiny, be disorganized, in Jesus' name.

Every demonic attack designed to terminate my health, fail woefully, in the name of Jesus. Almighty God, deliver me from every aggressive altar. Father Lord, boost my immunity spiritually and physically, in the name of Jesus. Blood of Jesus, close the door of my life forever from every satanic inversion. Heavenly father, arise and deliver me from every demonic sleep, in the name of Jesus.

Ancient of days, feed me with the food of the champions, in the name of Jesus. Father Lord, speak to me with the language I will understand, in the name of Jesus. Almighty God, open my eyes and ears to hear and see you in my dreams, in Jesus' name. Every enemy of God's dream for my destiny, be frustrated, in the name of Jesus. You my dream life under satanic attack, receive deliverance, in the name of Jesus. Anointing to recover every good thing I ever lost in my dreams, possess me, in Jesus' name.

Decrees for Deliverance from Dream Harasments

Every satanic initiation that took place in my dreams; I break away from you, in Jesus' name. I drink the blood of Jesus against every evil deposit in my body. Any defilement in my body, receive destruction by fire, in Jesus' name. Any evil personality that is assigned to defile me in the dream, perish. Any evil that took place in my past dreams, be terminated, in Jesus' name. I command every evil personality that has vowed to waste me in the dream to be wasted. O hand of God, take away every evil thing inside my life attracting satanic attacks, in Jesus' name.

Every evil planted into my life in the dream; be uprooted now. Blood of Jesus, neutralize all satanic poison in my life, in Jesus' name. Every sexual animal living inside my life; come out and die. Any sickness planted into my body in the dream, be destroyed from your root, in Jesus' name. Holy Ghost fire, burn to ashes every satanic poison in my system. Agent of dream criminal in my life, be frustrated. Every food I every ate in my dream through satanic source, expire, in the name of Jesus.

Let the fire of God enter into my body and destroy every evil work. Lord my God, deliver me from all evil activities in my dreams, in Jesus' name. Every evil structure in my body through evil dreams; burn to ashes. I command the dreams designed to divert my blessings to perish die force. Every evil dream causing me to lose God's blessings; I stop you, in Jesus' name. Every demonic organized sex in my dreams, fail woefully. Any part of my body that is already defiled; receive deliverance. Any dark room in my body, inhabiting problems, receive divine light now, in Jesus' name.

Any evil dream making me unclean, be terminated forever. Every power debasing me spiritually or physically; be debased, in Jesus' name. Every evil power from the waters, invading my life in the dream; I cast you out. I bring all sex in the dream come to an end forever, in Jesus' name. Almighty God, close my mouth against demonic food in the dream. Every evil force polluting my life in the dream, be terminated, in Jesus' name. Any evil altar receiving evil sacrifice against me, scatter. Wherever they will call my name for attacks in my dreams, blood of Jesus, answer for me, in Jesus' name. You the wall of my stomach receive immunity against evil food in the dream. Any evil voice speaking against me in the dream; be terminated, in Jesus' name.

Every demonic sex that took place in my life in the dream; die. I command the effect of evil drinks in my dreams to be frustrated, in Jesus' name. Holy Ghost power, arise and destroy every evil in my foundation. Every evil authority the enemy has over my life because of sex in my dream be terminated, in Jesus' name. Father Lord, commission me for victory over evil dream. I receive God's power to destroy evil dreams' investment, in Jesus' name.

Any dominating power assigned against me in my dreams, be wasted. Holy Ghost fire, charge my body against demonic dream deposits, in

Jesus' name. Any spiritual serpent in my life, come out now by force. I break and loose myself from every unrepentant evil dream, in Jesus' name. Any evil rivers flowing into my life in the dream; dry up. Every witchcraft power that has poisoned me in my dream; eat your poison, in Jesus' name. Lord Jesus, be enthroned in my dream life forever. Any siege of evil in my dreams; be broken to pieces, in Jesus' name. Fire of God, consume and burn to ashes every evil deposit in my bones. Father Lord, disappoint the enemies in my dream, in Jesus' name.

Any invitation given to the enemy into my life, I withdraw you now. Any satanic kitchen inside my life, receive destruction by fire, in Jesus' name. Father Lord, empower me to reign over dream defilers. Every evil authority in my dream that is eating me alive; die, in Jesus' name. Any evil programme going on at nights against me, be terminated. Lord Jesus, bring peace into my body against evil dream, in Jesus' name. Father Lord, arise and bring back my health lost in the dream. I swallow the oil of the Holy Ghost to destroy evil in my life, in Jesus' name.

Every strange fire burning in my life; quench by force in my life. I receive divine immunity against any evil dream, in my life, in Jesus' name. Any evil force that has captured my life through my dreams; I bind and cast you out. I bring the blood of Jesus against the consequences of evil dreams in my life, in Jesus' name. I smash the head of witchcraft animal that is living inside me. Any satanic filling station in my life; dry up by fire, in Jesus' name. Every enchantment against me in the battle field; backfire. I puncture every satanic balloon in my body, in Jesus' name.

I command divine lightning and thunderbolt destroy every evil inside my body. Every tragedy in my life from the dream; backfire, in Jesus' name. I recover double every good thing I had ever lost in my dreams. Every negative thing in my life through evil dreams, be terminated, in Jesus' name. Every satanic accusation against me in my dream; backfire. Every satanic weapon in my life from the dream; catch fire, burn to ashes, in Jesus' name.

Decrees for Deliverance from Dream Perversions

Almighty God, deliver me from every evil covenant and curse, in Jesus' name. Father Lord, close every satanic road into my life, spiritual and physical. Every evil dream repeating itself in my life, be terminated by fire, in Jesus' name. Father Lord, circle my life with the blood of Jesus against evil dreams. Almighty Father, deliver me from the grip of wicked dreams at nights, in Jesus' name. Any evil force that has arrested my dream life; scatter by force. Every power from the water that has vowed to waste my life; be wasted, in Jesus' name.

Any angel of darkness assigned against my dream life, be frustrated. Every witchcraft power, assisting the spirit of defilement in my dreams; die, in Jesus' name. I command every evil gang-up against my dream life to scatter in shame. I command every evil hideouts of the demons in my dream to be exposed, in Jesus' name. Any evil arrow of dream repetition in my life; I fire you back. Father Lord, arise and destroy the Goliath of repeated dream in my life, in Jesus' name.

Any enchantment, promoting repeated evil dreams in my life; expire. Father Lord, arise in your anger and end repeated dreams in my life, in Jesus' name. Evil powers of my father's house, in charge of the repetition of evil dreams, perish. Any curse placed upon my life by repetition of evil dreams, expire, in Jesus' name. I break and loose myself from every demonic dream repetition. Every evil power, feeding me in my dreams, your time is up, be destroyed, in Jesus' name. Father Lord, arise and deliver me from the power of repeated evil dreams. I break and loose my body organs from the attack of marine spirit dreams, in Jesus' name. Almighty God, give me divine immunity from every satanic inversion. I shall not surrender to evil dreams manipulators for any reason, in Jesus' name.

I close my mouth and every organ of my body from satanic dreams. Every stubborn enemy that has captured my dream life, be frustrated, in the name of Jesus. I command the dream that the enemy has vowed to use to destroy me to perish. Every marine witchcraft dream attacker against me; be disgraced now, in Jesus' name. Every affliction in my life as a result of repeated evil dreams, backfire. Any dream assigned to force evil into my life to destroy me; perish, in Jesus' name.

Any dream the enemy has decided to use on me; backfire. Every dream criminal on suicide mission against my life die alone, in Jesus' name. Altars of evil dreams in my life; scatter by divine wind now. I set ablaze the source of evil dreams in my life, in Jesus' name. Any satanic bungalow, housing the demon's dreams in my life; collapse. Blood of Jesus, flow into my foundation and deliver me from repeated evil dreams, in Jesus' name. Any evil growth in my body as a result of repeated evil dreams; die. Every evil movement in my life, catch the Holy Ghost fire, in Jesus' name. O Lord, arise and destroy all the works of repeated evil dreams. Anointing for divine sound health, fall upon me now, in Jesus' name.

Let the root of every evil in my life from the dream dry up. Any satanic witchcraft network to waste my life in the dream; fail woefully, in Jesus' name. Every conspiracy against my dream life; scatter. Every wisdom of my dream attackers; fail woefully now, in Jesus' name. Every demonic trap in my dreams, catch fire forever. Every evil padlock, locking up my destiny with dream attack; break into pieces, in Jesus' name.

Let every enemy of God's agenda for my life, be disgraced. The fear of dream attackers shall not waste my destiny, in Jesus' name. I use the power in the blood of Jesus to waste repeated evil dreams. Any area of my life under the attack of repeated evil dreams; be delivered, in Jesus' name. Every pregnancy of evil dream repetition; be miscarried. I receive divine boldness in my dreams to overcome every evil dream, in Jesus' name. Any evil dream that has enslaved my destiny; release me by force. Let that dream that repeats itself whenever am about to succeed, die, in Jesus' name.

Any satanic powers, working against my destiny through dream repetition; die. Blood of Jesus, speak repeated dreams out of my life, in Jesus' name. Any power that has risen against me in the dream; die. Any evil habit promoting repeated dreams in my life; be disgraced, in Jesus' name. Angels of the living God, arise and terminate repeated evil dreams in my life. Every covenant of the tail, taking me back to evil dreams; break, in Jesus' name. I receive perfect deliverance from repeated dreams. Blood of Jesus, flow into the roots of my life and destroy repeated dreams, in Jesus' name.

Father Lord, confront and conquer all forms of repeated evil dreams. Affliction of repeated evil dreams in my life; die, in Jesus name. By the power in the blood of Jesus, I shall arise above repeated evil dreams. Holy Ghost fire, consume the strength of evil repeated dreams in my life, in Jesus' name. Every consequence of repeated dream in my life; catch fire. Any evil power delegated to waste my star in the dream; be wasted, in Jesus' name.

Father Lord, make my life untouchable from evil occurrences in the dream. Let the giant of constant evil dream in my life, perish forever, in Jesus' name. Any evil altar bringing evil dreams into my life; catch fire. Every ancestral demon, bringing evil dreams into my life; I bind and cast you out, in Jesus' name. Let the evil sacrifice offered to attack my life in the dream, expire. Every good thing I have lost in my dream; I recover you double, in Jesus' name. Let the spirit of failures repeating itself in my dreams be terminated unto death. Any evil chain linking me up to evil dreams; break to pieces, in Jesus 'name.

I bind and cast out of my life the demon of repeated evil dreams. Every anti-peace in my dream life; be wasted, in Jesus' name. Let the hand of God cover me against evil dreams. Any power waiting for me to sleep to attack me; die and be burned, in Jesus' name. Any power blocking my prosperity in the dream; be removed forever, in my life. Any evil mouths swallowing my peace in the dream; vomit them and close your mouth forever, in Jesus' name. Any power that steals my blessings through evil dream; die. Any Jezebel of defilement in my dreams; fall down and die, in Jesus' name. Every messenger of evil dream; carry your message to your sender. Every serpent of demonic dream in my life; I cut off your head, in Jesus' name.

THANK YOU!

I wanted to take this opportunity to appreciate you for supporting my ministry and writing career by purchasing my book. I'm a full-time author and every copy of my book bought helps tremendously in supporting my family and that I continue to have the energy and motivation to write. My family and I are very grateful and we don't take your support lightly.

Thank you so much as you spare this precious moment of your time and may God bless you and meet you at every point of your need.

Send me an email on prayermadu@yahoo.com if you need prayers or counsel or you have questions. Better still if you want to be friends with me.

Other Books by Prayer Madueke

1. 100 Days Prayers to Wake Up Your Lazarus
2. 15 Deliverance Steps to Everlasting Life
3. 21/40 Nights of Decrees and Your Enemies Will Surrender
4. 35 Deliverance Steps to Everlasting Rest
5. 35 Special Dangerous Decrees
6. 40 Prayer Giants
7. Alone with God
8. Americans, May I Have Your Attention Please
9. Avoid Academic Defeats
10. Because You Are Living Abroad
11. Biafra of My Dream
12. Breaking Evil Yokes
13. Call to Renew Covenant
14. Command the Morning, Day and Night
15. Community Liberation and Solemn Assembly
16. Comprehensive Deliverance
17. Confront and Conquer Your Enemy
18. Contemporary Politicians' Prayers for Nation Building
19. Crossing the Hurdles
20. Dangerous Decrees to Destroy Your Destroyers (Series)
21. Dealing with Institutional Altars
22. Deliverance by Alpha and Omega
23. Deliverance from Academic Defeats

24. Deliverance from Compromise
25. Deliverance from Luke warmness
26. Deliverance from The Devil and His Agents
27. Deliverance from The Spirit of Jezebel
28. Deliverance Letters 1
29. Deliverance Letters 2
30. Deliverance Through Warning in Advance
31. Evil Summon
32. Foundation Exposed (Part 1)
33. Foundations Exposed (Part 2)
34. Healing Covenant
35. International Women's Prayer Network
36. Leviathan The Beast
37. Ministers Empowerment Prayer Network
38. More Kingdoms to Conquer
39. Organized Student in a Disorganized School
40. Pray for a New Nigeria
41. Pray for Jamaica
42. Pray for Trump, America, Israel and Yourself
43. Pray for Your Country
44. Pray for Your Pastor and Yourself
45. Prayer Campaign for a Better Ghana
46. Prayer Campaign for a Better Kenya
47. Prayer Campaign for Nigeria
48. Prayer Campaign for Uganda
49. Prayer Retreat
50. Prayers Against Premature Death

51. Prayers Against Satanic Oppression
52. Prayers for a Happy Married Life
53. Prayers for a Job Interview
54. Prayers for a Successful Career
55. Prayers for Academic Success
56. Prayers for an Excellent Job
57. Prayers for Breakthrough in Your Business
58. Prayers for Children and Youths
59. Prayers for Christmas
60. Prayers for College and University Students
61. Prayers for Conception and Power to Retain
62. Prayers for Deliverance
63. Prayers for Fertility in Your Marriage
64. Prayers for Financial Breakthrough
65. Prayers for Good Health
66. Prayers for Marriage and Family
67. Prayers for Marriages in Distress
68. Prayers for Mercy
69. Prayers for Nation Building
70. Prayers for Newly Married Couple
71. Prayers for Overcoming Attitude Problem
72. Prayers for Political Excellence and Veteran Politicians (Prayers for Nation Building Book 2)
73. Prayers for Pregnant Women
74. Prayers for Restoration of Peace in Marriage
75. Prayers for Sound Sleep and Rest
76. Prayers for Success in Examination

77. Prayers for Widows and Orphans
78. Prayers for Your Children's Deliverance
79. Prayers to Buy a Home and Settle Down
80. Prayers to Conceive and Bear Children
81. Prayers to Deliver Your Child Safely
82. Prayers to End a Prolonged Pregnancy
83. Prayers to Enjoy Your Wealth and Riches
84. Prayers to Experience Love in Your Marriage
85. Prayers to Get Married Happily
86. Prayers to Heal Broken Relationship
87. Prayers to Keep Your Marriage Out of Trouble
88. Prayers to Live an Excellent Life
89. Prayers to Live and End Your Life Well
90. Prayers to Marry Without Delay
91. Prayers to Overcome an Evil Habit
92. Prayers to Overcome Attitude Problems
93. Prayers to Overcome Miscarriage
94. Prayers to Pray During Honeymoon
95. Prayers to Preserve Your Marriage
96. Prayers to Prevent Separation of Couples
97. Prayers to Progress in Your Career
98. Prayers to Raise Godly Children
99. Prayers to Receive Financial Miracle
100. Prayers to Retain Your Pregnancy
101. Prayers to Triumph Over Divorce
102. Queen of Heaven: Wife of Satan
103. School for Children Teachers

104. School for Church Workers
105. School for Women of Purpose: Women
106. School for Youths and Students
107. School of Deliverance with Eternity in View
108. School of Ministry for Ministers in Ministry
109. School of Prayer
110. Speaking Things into Existence (Series)
111. Special Prayers in His Presence
112. Tears in Prison: Prisoners of Hope
113. The First Deliverance
114. The Operation of the Woman That Sit Upon Many Waters
115. The Philosophy of Deliverance
116. The Reality of Spirit Marriage
117. The Sword of New Testament Deliverance
118. Two Prosperities
119. Upon All These Prayers
120. Veteran Politicians' Prayers for Nation Building
121. Welcome to Campus
122. When Evil Altars Are Multiplied
123. When I Grow Up Visions
124. You Are a Man's Wife
125. Your Dream Directory
126. *Youths, May I Have Your Attention Please?*

Free Book Gift

Just to say Thank You for getting my book: Divine Protection and Immunity while Sleeping, I'll like to give you these books for free:

Click here to download these books now

If you're reading this from the paperback version, email me at prayermadu@yahoo.com.

Your testimonies will abound. Click here to see my other books. They have produced many testimonies and I want your testimony to be one too.

An Invitation to Become a Ministry Partner

In response to several calls from readers of my books on how to partner with this ministry, we are grateful to provide our ministry's bank details.

Be assured that our continued prayers for you will be answered according to God's word, and as you remain faithful by sowing seeds of faith, God will never forget your labors of love in Christ.

Send your Seed to:

In Nigeria & Africa

Bank Name: Access Bank

Account Name: Prayer Emancipation Missions

Account Number: 0692638220

In the United States & the rest of the World

Bank Name: Bank of America

Account Name: Roseline C Madueke

Account Number: 483079070578

Routing Number (RTN): 021000322

Visit the donation page on my website to donate online: www.madueke.com/donate.

Made in the USA
Columbia, SC
18 September 2023